CANADA
PAST · PRESENT · FUTURE

FRENCH-ENGLISH RELATIONS

BY STEVE GOLDSWORTHY

Weigl

Published by Weigl Educational Publishers Limited
6325 10th Street SE
Calgary, Alberta, Canada T2H 2Z9
Website: www.weigl.com

Library and Archives Canada Cataloguing in Publication data available upon request.
Fax (403) 233-7769 for the attention of the Publishing Records department.

ISBN 978-1-55388-690-7 (hard cover)
ISBN 978-1-55388-695-2 (soft cover)

Printed in the United States of America in North Mankato, Minnesota
1 2 3 4 5 6 7 8 9 0 14 13 12 11 10

072010
WEP230610

All of the Internet URLs given in the book were valid at the time of publication. However, due to the dynamic nature of the Internet, some addresses may have changed, or sites may have ceased to exist since publication. While the author and publisher regret any inconvenience this may cause readers, no responsibility for any such changes can be accepted by either the author or the publisher.

Weigl acknowledges Getty Images and Library and Archives Canada as its image suppliers for this title.

Every reasonable effort has been made to trace ownership and to obtain permission to reprint copyright material. The publishers would be pleased to have any errors or omissions brought to their attention so that they may be corrected in subsequent printings.

We gratefully acknowledge the financial support of the Government of Canada through the Canada Book Fund for our publishing activities.

EDITOR: Aaron Carr
DESIGN: Terry Paulhus

French-English Relations
Contents

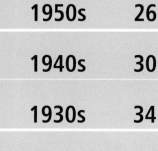

Through The Years

The history of French-English relations in Canada is older than the country itself. Before Canada became a nation, French and British colonies existed side-by-side in the area. The founding of Canada was a direct result of French-English relations. In 1759, French and British colonial forces fought on the Plains of Abraham to determine the geographic and political basis of Canada. Decades later, the region was divided into Upper Canada and Lower Canada. Upper Canada later became Ontario, and Lower Canada became Quebec.

French-English relations have often been strained. There have been many debates, votes, and **referendums** on topics ranging from Francophone, or French-speaking, rights and language laws to Quebec's separation from Canada. Leaders such as Louis Riel and Sir Wilfrid Laurier have guided French-English relations. French-Canadian journalist Henri Bourassa promoted a unified Canada that embraced both French and English language and culture.

Later, Prime Minister Pierre Elliott Trudeau made Bourassa's dream a reality by granting both languages official status. Canada's ongoing French-English relations are a sign of a healthy democracy.

Debate is the cornerstone of a free society. If two sides can come together with honesty and respect, great things can be achieved. Canada's seventh prime minister, Sir Wilfrid Laurier, once wrote, "Two races share today the soil of Canada....These people had not always been friends. But I hasten to say it....There is no longer any family here but the human family. It matters not the language people speak, or the altars at which they kneel." Canada's history of French-English relations helped shape it into a nation based on the idea of multiculturalism. This means people of all languages and cultures can call themselves Canadian.

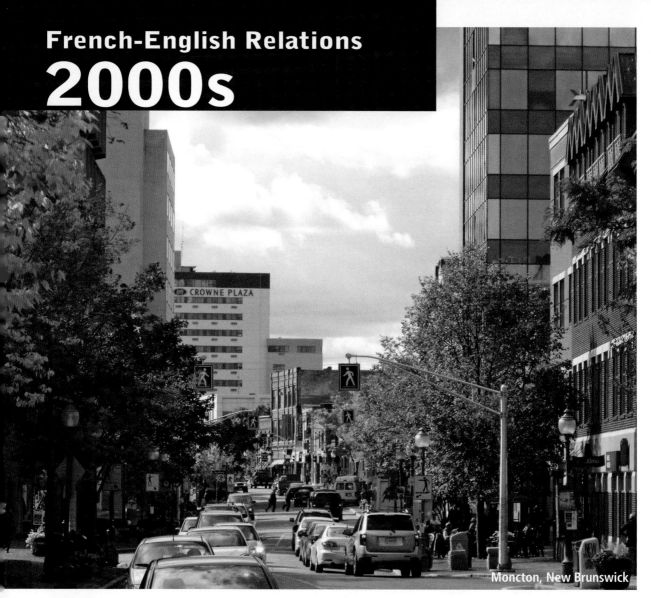

Moncton, New Brunswick

2002

Moncton, New Brunswick

The fast-growing city of Moncton, New Brunswick, has a strong French-English history. Originally settled by **Acadians** in the 1730s, the first English-speaking settlers arrived from Pennsylvania about 30 years later. The area was called The Bend until 1855, when it was incorporated into a town and named after British Lieutenant-Colonel Robert Monckton. It grew as a railroad town for more than a century until the closure of the Canadian National Railway's locomotive shops in 1988. Moncton's resilience comes from its diversity and ability to adapt. It was this diversity that led to Moncton becoming the first officially **bilingual** city in Canada in 2002. People who speak English as their first language make up 64 percent of the Moncton population. The city also has a vibrant French-speaking Acadian population that accounts for 34 percent of the city's people. Almost 40 percent of the city's population is bilingual.

2001

A New Brunswick court rules that all municipal laws must be enacted in both French and English.

2002

Moncton, New Brunswick, becomes Canada's first officially bilingual city.

Jean Charest

Quebec Language

2006

Quebec Language

The official language of Quebec is French. Quebec is the only province in Canada with a primarily Francophone population. According to a 2006 census, 80 percent of the population considered French their first language, about 8 percent declared English as their first language, and about 12 percent cited a language other than French or English. About 40 percent of Quebec's population consider themselves bilingual. Most of Quebec's bilingual population live in Montreal, where the bilingual percentage is about 54 percent. Outside the province, only 10 percent of Canadians are bilingual.

2003

Jean Charest

Quebec premier Bernard Landry lost the 2003 election to the Quebec Liberal Party and its leader Jean Charest. The victory made Charest the second liberal Quebec premier in more than 30 years. John James "Jean" Charest was born on June 24, 1958, in Sherbrooke, Quebec. He worked as a lawyer until 1984, when he was elected to Parliament as a member of the federal Progressive Conservative Party. At age 28, Charest was appointed to the cabinet as minister of state for youth, which made him the youngest cabinet minister in Canadian history. In 1995, he gained the leadership of the Progressive Conservative Party. Charest left federal politics in 1998 to become leader of the Quebec Liberal Party (QLP). He was considered the party's best hope to defeat the ruling Parti Québécois. In 2003, Charest led the QLP to a majority government.

2003

A survey says having two official languages makes 75 percent of Francophones proud to be Canadian.

2004

July 28 becomes the official day to remember Acadian history.

2005

The Conservative Party states Canada's official languages "benefit all Canadians."

French-English Canadian Cinema

Canadian filmmaking dates back to the silent era, when movies did not have sound. In 1897, Manitoba farmer James Freer made documentaries of his home province to promote living on the Canadian Prairies to Europeans. Through government-run institutions, such as the National Film Board of Canada, both French and English cinema have found an audience. English-based theatres have been dominated by American cinema. Homegrown Canadian English language films make up only 1.1 percent of the box office. However, French language films have great success in Quebec, accounting for 26 percent of the provincial box office. While many of these films do not have much success outside the province, others have earned great international acclaim. In 2003, *Les Invasions Barb* (*The Barbarian Invasions*) won the Academy Award for best foreign language film, while *Le Déclin de l'empire américain*, (*The Decline of the American Empire*) and *Jésus de Montréal* (*Jesus of Montreal*) had previously received Academy Award nominations.

French-English Canadian Cinema

2006

The federal government recognizes the Québecois as a nation within a united Canada.

2007

Bon Cop, Bad Cop wins a Genie Award for best picture.

2008

French-Canadian singer Celine Dion becomes the best-selling female artist of all time.

Acadians Remembered

In 2003, the Société Saint-Thomas d'Aquin of Prince Edward Island named December 13 Acadian Remembrance Day in the province. This day was set aside to remember the sinking of the *Duke William*, the *Violet*, and a third ship of unknown name. The three ships were attempting to carry an estimated 2,000 Acadians to safety in France. From 1755 to 1763, Acadians were deported from their settlements in the Maritimes. This event was known as the Great Expulsion. In 2004, the Government of Canada issued a statement acknowledging the deportation of Acadians. July 28 became a national day to remember the event.

Acadians Remembered

Into the Future

In the 2006 census, 42.4 percent of Francophones said they were able to conduct a conversation in English and French. In Quebec, about 40 percent of Francophones reported being bilingual. The majority of Francophones living outside Quebec, 83.6 percent, were bilingual. In Quebec, 68.9 percent of Anglophone, or English-speaking, Canadians speak both English and French, while 7.4 percent of Anglophones outside Quebec said they could carry on a conversation in both official languages. Do you live in a mainly French or English community? How has exposure to another language enriched your own life?

2009

The Supreme Court rules New Brunswick RCMP must be bilingual.

2010

The Olympic Winter Games are held in Vancouver, British Columbia, with ceremonies showcasing French and English Canadian culture.

The Bloc Québécois

1991

The Bloc Québécois

The **sovereigntist** Bloc Québécois party was formed in Ottawa over the defeat of the Meech Lake Accord, an attempt to **amend** the Constitution in order to gain Quebec's support. Quebec members of Parliament from both the federal Progressive Conservative and Liberal parties left their respective parties to form the Bloc. Led by Lucien Bouchard, former Conservative minister of the environment, they formed a party to protect the rights of Quebec language and culture. The party fights for the province's independence from the rest of Canada. The Bloc gained official party status in 1991. The first Bloc candidate elected to the House of Commons was Gilles Duceppe. The Bloc won 54 seats in the 1993 federal election, becoming the official opposition in the House of Commons. Because both groups were in favour of Quebec separating from Canada, the federal Bloc Québécois and the provincial Parti Québécois (PQ) often supported each other. In the 1995 provincial referendum on Quebec sovereignty, the Bloc worked with the PQ to campaign for the "Yes" side of the vote. Those who voted "Yes" wanted Quebec to become a sovereign nation, while those who voted "No" wanted the province to remain a part of Canada. After the "No" side won, Premier Jacques Parizeau stepped down, and Bouchard gave up his seat in Parliament. Bouchard then joined the PQ and took over as premier of Quebec. Gilles Duceppe later replaced Bouchard as the leader of the Bloc Québécois.

1991
The Dobbie-Castonguay Commission recommends distinct society status for Quebec.

1992
The Charlottetown Accord fails.

1993
The Bloc Québécois forms the official opposition in the House of Commons.

1995

Second Quebec Sovereignty Referendum

After nearly a decade of Liberal leadership in Quebec, the Parti Québécois was voted back into power in 1994. Premier Jacques Parizeau and the PQ called a second referendum on sovereignty on October 30, 1995. They posed a new question to the citizens of Quebec. They asked, "Do you agree that Québec should become sovereign after having made a formal offer to Canada for a new economic and political partnership within the scope of the bill respecting the future of Québec and of the agreement signed on June 12, 1995?" The question was criticized as confusing to some people. They wondered if it was asking if they thought Quebec should separate from the rest of Canada, or if it was asking if they wanted a better deal with the rest of Canada. The main proponent on the "No" side of the vote was federalist and Quebec Liberal Party leader Daniel Johnson.

The head of the "Yes" side was Parizeau himself. As the campaign to persuade Quebecers continued, support for the "Yes" side, or those in favour of separation from Canada, grew. This sparked massive rallies across the country as the rest of Canada pleaded with Quebec to stay part of the country. Finally, the people of Quebec voted "No" on the referendum by a slim margin of 50.58 percent to 49.42 percent. The closeness of the result represented the passion Quebecers have for their country and their province.

1994

The Parti Québécois returns to power under Premier Jacques Parizeau.

1995

Premier Jacques Parizeau tables the Sovereignty Bill asserting Quebec's independent rights.

Gilles Duceppe

Gilles Duceppe

On March 15, 1997, Gilles Duceppe was elected leader of the Bloc Québécois. Duceppe was born on July 22, 1947, in Montreal, Quebec. Inspired by René Lévesque and his ideas of a sovereignty-association between Canada and Quebec, Duceppe became a sovereigntist at the age of 20. He was politically active throughout his college years before joining the Bloc Québécois. In 1990, he was elected to the Canadian House of Commons as an **independent**. In 1996, Lucien Bouchard stepped down as leader of the Bloc, handing the leadership briefly to Duceppe. Later, Michel Gauthier was voted leader of the Bloc, but he was soon removed by dissatisfied members. Duceppe took over leadership of the party, as well as the role of leader of the opposition in Parliament. Duceppe continued to fight for Quebec sovereignty in Parliament. In the 2006 federal election, Duceppe and the Bloc Québécois lost Official Opposition status to the Liberal Party. However, Duceppe continued to lobby for a separate Quebec.

1996

Lucien Bouchard becomes premier of Quebec.

1997

All items sold in Quebec must now come with French packaging and instruction manuals.

1998

The Supreme Court rules Quebec needs federal approval to separate from Canada.

1999

The Francophonie Summit

From September 3 to 5, Moncton, New Brunswick, was host to the Francophonie Summit. Heads of state from 54 member nations attended the conference to celebrate and promote French language and culture throughout the world. Member Nations included France, Belgium, Haiti, Republic of the Congo, and Vanuatu. The summit was created in 1970, adopting the motto *égalité, complémentarité, solidarité*, which means "equality, complementarity, and solidarity." A small number of countries made up the first membership. It soon grew into a global organization with a mandate of co-operating among members in the fields of culture, economy, science, and promotion of peace. The Francophonie Summit of 1999 established Moncton as a city capable of hosting a large international event. At a time when the city's economy was in turmoil, the summit bolstered the confidence of Moncton's citizens. This helped the city begin its economic recovery, echoing the city's motto *Resurgo*, which is Latin for "I rise again."

Into the Future

In 1991, the Citizen's Forum on Canada's Future created a report on the state of French-English relations in Canada. The report stated, "Canada's use of two official languages is widely seen as a fundamental and distinctive Canadian characteristic." Do you speak both official languages? What benefits do you see in being able to speak both English and French?

1999

The Clarity Act proposes conditions under which a province can vote to leave Canada.

2000

The Supreme Court rules that equal access to education in either official language must be provided across the country.

Quebec Referendum

1980

Quebec Referendum

The first Quebec referendum on sovereignty and Quebec's place in Canada was held on May 20, 1980. Premier René Lévesque and his Parti Québécois government called the referendum. The PQ had always favoured Quebec's separation from the rest of Canada. The party sought exclusive power over laws, taxes, and international affairs for Quebec but wanted to maintain an economic association with Canada, including a common currency. The referendum sought the approval of Quebec citizens to negotiate this proposed agreement between Quebec and Canada. There was heavy campaigning for the "Yes" and "No" side. Prime Minister Pierre Elliott Trudeau promised to make changes to the Canadian Constitution if the "No" side won. When the votes were counted, the "No" side won by a margin of 59.56 percent to 40 percent. Two years later, Trudeau successfully passed a new Constitution in the House of Commons. Quebec, however, refused to sign it.

1981

The Parti Québécois is re-elected in Quebec.

1982

Alliance Quebec is formed to represent English-speaking Quebecers.

1983

Quebec's Charter of the French Language is amended to recognize Anglophone institutions.

1982

Constitution Act

Prime Minister Trudeau succeeded in patriating the Canadian Constitution with the Constitution Act of 1982. Great Britain's Queen Elizabeth signed a proclamation bringing the act into effect on April 17, 1982. The Canadian Charter of Rights and Freedoms makes up the first 35 sections of the act. The charter protects certain political and civil rights of Canadian citizens. It also unifies them around a set of principles to uphold those rights. One of those principles is the idea of a bilingual society. Section 16(1) of the Charter of Rights and Freedoms states that English and French will have "equality of status, and equal rights and privileges as to their use in all institutions of the Parliament and Government of Canada." Since 1982, all provinces except Quebec have formally approved the act. Though consent from all provinces is not needed, there have been several attempts to amends the Constitution to gain Quebec's support since 1982.

1981

The Kitchen Accord

In an attempt to **patriate** the Constitution of Canada, Prime Minister Trudeau met with nine of the 10 provincial premiers in the kitchen of the Chateau Laurier hotel in Ottawa on November 4, 1981. Quebec Premier René Lévesque was not at the meeting because he refused to stay at the hotel. The late night meeting was negotiated by Federal Justice Minister Jean Chrétien, Attorney General of Saskatchewan Roy Romanow, and Attorney General of Ontario Roy McMurtry. The goal of the meeting was to come to an agreement between the federal government and each of the provincial governments concerning changes to the Constitution. After hours of negotiating, all members present signed the document. This effectively approved the Constitution Act of 1982 in all provinces except Quebec. The next morning, Bouchard was presented with the signed document. He refused to sign it and returned to Quebec. This meeting became known in Quebec as *La nuit des longs couteaux*, or "the Night of Long Knives." In the rest of Canada, it was known as the Kitchen Accord. Years later, Lucien Bouchard wrote about the event. He said, "Perceived as trickery in Quebec, the repatriation of 1982 has placed a time bomb in the political dynamics of this country."

Constitution Act

1984

The Northwest Territories grants official status to English, French, and nine aboriginal languages.

1985

The Supreme Court rules laws in Manitoba cannot be in English only.

Meech Lake Accord

Prime Minister Brian Mulroney attempted to amend the 1982 Canadian Constitution to gain endorsement from the province of Quebec. It was hoped this would increase support in Quebec to remain a part of Canada. Although the Supreme Court ruled that no one province had the right to veto, or overrule, the Constitution by not signing it, Quebec's refusal to sign in 1982 was seen as a strain on relations with the rest of Canada. However, with Brian Mulroney's election as prime minister of Canada, and Robert Bourassa's election as premier of Quebec, things looked optimistic. The Meech Lake Accord was negotiated at a meeting between the prime minister and the provincial premiers at a place called Wilson House on Meech Lake in the Gatineau Hills of Quebec. The accord included several modifications to the Canadian Constitution, including recognizing Quebec as a "distinct society" and a constitutional veto for Quebec. Mulroney referred to the accord as the "Quebec round." All 10 provincial premiers agreed to the accord, but public opinion soon turned against it. Many people thought the term "distinct society" meant granting Quebec special status. Years of political renegotiation began. The accord officially failed in 1990, in response to public demand and concerns raised from Canada's Aboriginal Peoples.

Meech Lake Accord

1986	1987	1988
Law 142 urges Quebec health and social services to offer English service.	René Lévesque dies of a heart attack.	In Quebec, the Supreme Court rules that Bill 101's ban of English signs is illegal.

Official Languages Act

The Official Languages Act was amended in 1988 to correct omissions from the original Official Languages Act of 1969. Changes to the act included giving equal status to English and French in the Government of Canada. This means Canadians now have the right to receive services from federal departments in both official languages. Under the act, federal court cases may be heard in either English or French. The act also states that all laws and public regulations must be published in both official languages, and both English and French must be spoken by federal public service employees. With the amendment, the position of Commissioner of Official Languages was created. This officer of Parliament's job is to receive language related complaints from the public, investigate language issues, and make recommendations regarding the two official languages. The Official Languages Act protects the minority language speaking citizens of each province. It is the primary legislation for official bilingualism in Canada.

Official Languages Act

Into the Future

Queen Elizabeth II signed the Constitution Act into law in 1982. The constitution is a powerful tool of Canada's democracy. It is used to ensure the rights and freedoms of all Canadian citizens. Consider your own rights and freedoms. Which do you cherish the most? What other principles do you think make your country a better place to live?

1989

A Nova Scotia court rules that laws must be explained in both official languages.

1990

Three Francophone Albertans win their fight for improved minority language education.

1970s

The October Crisis

Pierre Elliott Trudeau

1970

The October Crisis

On October 5, 1970, a radical Quebec nationalist group, the Front de libération du Québec (FLQ), kidnapped British Trade Commissioner James Cross in Montreal. On October 10, Quebec's Minister of Labour, Pierre Laporte, was also kidnapped by the group. The FLQ had a list of demands, including the reading of their **manifesto** on the radio and the release of several convicted FLQ members from jail. The terrorist act set off several demonstrations throughout Quebec. Most people condemned the kidnappings, but others saw them as a chance to once again debate Quebec's sovereignty. Quebec premier Robert Bourassa asked the federal government to grant his province emergency powers. It marked the only peacetime usage of the **War Measures Act** in Canadian history. Through the act, Quebec police officers were allowed to arrest and detain individuals without charging them with a crime. Quebec police started a massive investigation that led to the hideout where Cross was being held. The police raided the FLQ hideout and rescued Cross. However, Laporte's body was later found in the trunk of a car. After years of investigation, Quebec police arrested Laporte's murderers. They were tried and convicted for their crimes. The crisis brought many French- and English-speaking Canadians together as they sought peaceful ways to settle their differences.

1971

Prime Minister Trudeau attempts to amend the Constitution with the Victoria Charter.

1972

Trudeau and the federal Liberal Party win a second term on October 30.

Cereal Box Bilingualism

1972

Pierre Elliott Trudeau

Pierre Elliott Trudeau was born October 18, 1919, in Montreal, Quebec. After earning a law degree from the Université de Montréal in 1943, Trudeau was **conscripted** into the Canadian Army, though he was not sent overseas to fight in World War II. He then attended Harvard and studied economics abroad in Paris and London. Back in Montreal, Trudeau co-founded the left-wing newspaper Cité Libre. The newspaper was known for criticizing then Premier Maurice Duplessis. When Trudeau entered federal politics, it was as a member of the Liberal Party. In 1967, Trudeau became Canada's minister of justice and would later introduce the Criminal Law Amendment Act in 1968. This was the largest amendment ever made to the Canadian criminal code at one time. Despite being new to the Liberal Party, Trudeau was elected leader of the Liberals in April 1968. Later that year, Prime Minister Lester B. Pearson resigned. Trudeau won the federal election on June 25, 1968, on a wave of popularity many called "Trudeaumania." He introduced reforms to healthcare, justice, education, and citizens' rights. Trudeau passed legislation making all Canadian federal institutions officially bilingual and drafted patriation of the Canadian Constitution in 1982. He led Canada through many key events in Canadian history, including the October Crisis of 1970 and the Quebec sovereignty referendum of 1980. Trudeau retired from politics in 1984.

1974

Cereal Box Bilingualism

In 1974, the Canadian government enacted the Consumer Packaging and Labelling Act, which required the use of both French and English on all consumer packaging across the country. This gave bilingualism in Canada a real boost. Many schoolchildren began to learn French or English from common household items. This prompted some people to call the phenomenon "cereal box bilingualism." Children learned terms such as "flocons de maïs" for Corn Flakes, "pamplemousse" for grapefruit, or "jus de pomme" for apple juice. Bilingual packaging has become a part of everyday life in Canada.

1973

Civil servants can now work in either official language.

1974

Quebec enacts the Official Language Act.

1975

Quebec passes the Charter of Human Rights and Freedoms.

René Lévesque

1976

René Lévesque

On November 15, 1976, René Lévesque and the Parti Québécois (PQ) won the Quebec provincial election. Lévesque was born August 24, 1922, in Campbellton, New Brunswick, and raised in New Carlisle, Quebec. During World War II, he became a war correspondent for local radio stations and newspapers. During the Korean War, Lévesque worked for the Canadian Broadcasting Corporation's (CBC) French-language branch, Radio-Canada. In 1960, he entered Quebec politics as minister of hydroelectric resources and public works. He left the Quebec Liberal Party in 1967 and founded the Mouvement Souveraineté-Association, which later merged with the Ralliement National to form the PQ in 1968. In 1976, Lévesque and the PQ swept the provincial election, and Lévesque became premier. In his 11 years in office, Lévesque passed the Quebec Charter of the French Language, called a province-wide referendum of Quebec sovereignty, and continued his fight for an independent Quebec. He resigned from the PQ on June 20, 1985, feeling the party was putting too much emphasis on sovereignty. Lévesque died suddenly of a heart attack on November 1, 1987. A controversial and passionate politician, he remains respected by his peers and thought of by many as a hero in Quebec.

1976

Richard Rohmer's novel *Separation*, a fictional story of a Quebec attempt to separate from Canada, is published.

1977

Quebec Premier René Lévesque introduces the Charter of the French Language.

University of Moncton

The Université de Moncton, or University of Moncton, was founded in 1963. It is the only French-speaking university in New Brunswick. The university was created to serve the growing needs of the Francophone population outside of Quebec, particularly Acadians. The university consists of six colleges and several faculties, including arts and social science, engineering, health science, and education. With language laws changing, the need for French-speaking lawyers for clients outside of Quebec was rising. In response, the University of Moncton's Faculty of Law was founded in 1978. It is one of only two exclusively French universities in the Maritime provinces.

University of Moncton

Into the Future

The Canadian government learned much about handling conflicts during the 1970s. During the October Crisis, Prime Minister Trudeau went to great lengths to restore peace and rescue the hostages. What are some other ways people can resolve their differences? What do you do when faced with conflict?

1978

Canada's criminal code is amended to give people the right to be heard by a judge who speaks their language.

1979

The Quebec government publishes *Québec-Canada: A New Deal*.

1980

Prime Minister Trudeau is re-elected.

The Quiet Revolution

1960s

The Quiet Revolution

In the 1960s, a period of great change began in Quebec. This period was referred to as the *Révolution tranquille*, or "**Quiet Revolution**." The era began with the provincial election of Jean Lesage and the Liberal Party after the death of former premier Maurice Duplessis.

Duplessis's premiership was often referred to as the Grande Noirceur, or "Great Darkness." Lesage brought reform to all levels of government, including the transfer of control from church to state in regards to education and health, as well as the establishment of a **welfare** state. The Quiet Revolution also marked a split between Quebec federalists and separatists. The

revolution saw the formation of the sovereigntist Parti Québécois, René Lévesque's rise to power, as well as terrorist activity by the FLQ. This period also included the signing of the Charter of French Language. The charter sought to protect the French language and restrict English use in business, such as store signs.

1961

The Quebec Office of the French Language is established in Quebec.

1962

Activist groups form in Quebec to protest in the name of Quebec sovereignty.

1960

National Independence

The *Rassemblement pour l'indépendance nationale*, or "Rally for National Independence" (RIN), was founded on September 10, 1960, at the beginning of the Quiet Revolution. This highly conservative group rallied for the national independence of Quebec as a sovereign state. The RIN became a political party in 1963, and in 1964, Pierre Bourgault became its leader. As a party, the RIN participated in a number of demonstrations, including a protest of Queen Elizabeth II's visit to Quebec in 1964. In the 1966 provincial Quebec election, the RIN, together with the Ralliement National, won 8.8 percent of the popular vote but did not win a seat. This was encouraging to members and their idea of an independent Quebec. When

René Lévesque left the Liberals to form his own party in 1967, the Ralliement national quickly negotiated a merger. A balance was struck between the right-wing, or conservative, values of the Ralliement National, and the left-wing ideals of Lévesque. This merger led to the creation of the Parti Québécois in 1968. The RIN then voted to dissolve the party and join the PQ.

1963

The FLQ

The Front de liberation du Quebec (FLQ) was an extreme left-wing organization that took a stand for the complete independence of Quebec. It was active between 1963 and 1970. The FLQ was in favour of using violence to aid its cause. As a result, the FLQ was considered a terrorist group. The FLQ was founded by three former RIN members, Georges Schoeters, Raymond Villeneuve, and Gabriel Hudon. The FLQ participated in bank robberies, bombings, and kidnappings. Their crimes resulted in the deaths of eight people and the injuries of many more. Their terror activities reached a peak with the October Crisis in 1970. When the crisis came to an end, the FLQ disintegrated as its members were either arrested or abandoned the cause.

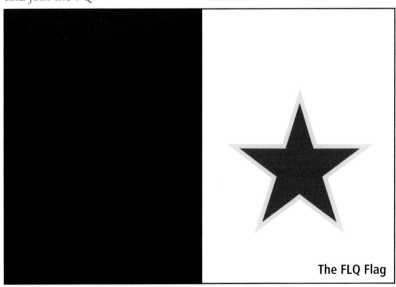

The FLQ Flag

1963
The Royal Commission on Bilingualism and Biculturalism is formed.

1964
Trans-Canada Airlines is renamed Air Canada.

1965
The conservative Ralliement national becomes a political party in Quebec.

23

"Vive le Quebec libre!"

1967

"Vive le Québec libre!"

While on a visit to Montreal in June 1967, French President Charles de Gaulle proclaimed, *"Vive le Québec libre!"* This means, "Long live free Quebec!" His words sparked an international controversy. President de Gaulle, who had granted independence to Algeria, shouted the words during a speech from the balcony of Montreal's city hall. He was on an official visit to Canada, but instead of arriving at the country's capital, which was standard procedure, he instead arrived in Quebec City. Days later, he travelled to Montreal. His mention of a free Quebec offended the federal government.

Many English-speaking Canadians felt it was an insult to Canadian soldiers who died on the battlefields of France in World Wars I and II. The visit was cut short, and de Gaulle left the country. However, many Quebec sovereigntists saw his declaration as support for their right to separate from Canada.

1968

The Parti Québécois

The Parti Québécois was founded in 1968 as a provincial party that aimed to promote Quebec sovereignty and separation from the rest of Canada. The PQ began when the *Mouvement Souveraineté-Association*, led by René Lévesque, merged with the Ralliement national party.

Lévesque then assumed leadership. The PQ was elected in 1976 to form the provincial government of Quebec. Most Francophones saw the election of the PQ and Premier Lévesque as a victory, while many Anglophones saw it as a threat. As a result, many English–speaking residents moved to nearby centres, such as Toronto. In 1977, the PQ passed the Charter of the French Language, affirming French as the only official language of the province. The charter also forbade immigrants and Quebecers of French descent from attending public English-language schools. In 1984, Lévesque resigned. The PQ lost the provincial election to Robert Bourassa and the Liberal Party in 1985. In 1995, the PQ regained leadership with Jacques Parizeau as premier. The PQ called the 1980 and 1995 referendums on Quebec sovereignty. Both were defeated.

The Parti Québécois

1966

Manitoba schools reintroduce French-language instruction.

1967

The World's Fair comes to Montreal for Expo '67.

1968

The Education Act in Ontario is amended to recognize French-language schools.

1969

Bilinigual New Brunswick

Bilingual New Brunswick

In 1969, the New Brunswick provincial government enacted its first Official Languages Act. The act granted "equality of status and equal rights and privileges as to their use" to both French and English. This made New Brunswick the first, and only, province to become officially bilingual. The same year, Prime Minister Trudeau passed an act to make both French and English official languages in all federal institutions. New Brunswick began amending its laws to guarantee equal status and rights to both languages in 1960 under Premier Louis Robichaud. The province is mainly English-speaking, but there is a large Francophone community that accounts for about 33 percent of the population. New Brunswick Francophones are mainly of Acadian descent. French has been an important part of New Brunswick's history since the province was first explored by Jacques Cartier in 1534. Over the next 150 years, the entire maritime region, including Nova Scotia, Prince Edward Island, and parts of the U.S. state of Maine, was proclaimed the French colony of Acadia. From 1756 to 1763, French settlers fought British colonialism in the Seven Years War. During the war, the British forced Acadians to leave the area. It was not until the early 19th century that some Acadians settled in what is now New Brunswick.

Into the Future

New Brunswick Premier Louis Robichaud said, "Language rights are more than legal rights. They are precious cultural rights, going deep into the revered past and touching the historic traditions of all our people." History is important to understanding French-English relations. Every person has a history. This history shapes their identity. What is your family history? Do you have English or French heritage? Explore your family history, and discover the language of your past.

1969

Canada adopts its first Official Languages Act, making English and French official languages.

1970

The Ontario government creates a new post to oversee government services in French.

Mackenzie King Dies

1950

Mackenzie King Dies

William Lyon Mackenzie King was Canada's longest-serving prime minister. He was born December 17, 1874, in what is now Kitchener, Ontario. King was the grandson of Toronto's first mayor and leader of the 1837 Upper Canada Rebellion, William Lyon Mackenzie. In 1900, after earning five university degrees, King became a civil servant in Ottawa. He became Canada's first minister of labour in 1909 and was soon elected to Parliament as a member of the Liberal Party. There, King worked to improve the lives of Canadian workers. He lost his seat in 1911 when the Conservative Party defeated the Liberals. King then went to work with the Rockefeller Foundation, a charitable organization, in New York City. Later, he went on to work as a consultant to various American corporations. When Liberal leader Wilfrid Laurier died in 1919, King was elected as his successor. King could not speak French, but he had powerful allies in Quebec. As a result, the Liberals won the election in 1921, and King became prime minister. He led Canada through the Great Depression and World War II. During this time, King also worked for Canada's right to govern itself independent of Great Britain. In 1948, he retired after 22 years as prime minister. King died on July 22, 1950.

1951

The Massey Report recommends government changes to protect Canadian culture.

1952

Henri Bourassa dies in Outremont, Quebec.

1953

The National Library of Canada is founded, based on the Massey Report.

Henri Bourassa Dies

Joseph-Napoléon-Henri Bourassa was a French-Canadian politician and publisher. Bourassa was born on September 1, 1868, in Montreal, Quebec. He became mayor of Montebello, Quebec, at the age of 22. In 1896, Bourassa was elected to the House of Commons as an independent liberal, but resigned in protest in 1899 over Canada's involvement in the Boer War. Bourassa was soon re-elected, and in 1903, he created the Nationalist League to promote Canadian national pride in Francophone citizens. He pushed for Canada's political independence from the British. In 1907, Bourassa left federal politics but continued to be a strong critic of Prime Minister Wilfrid Laurier. In an effort to promote the Nationalist League, Bourassa founded the newspaper *Le Devoir* in 1910. He served as editor of the publication until 1932. Bourassa continued to fight for French rights in other parts of Canada, criticizing the Ontario government in 1913 for wanting to ban the use of French in schools. He was a strong opponent of conscription during Word War I. While he did feel the war in Europe was necessary, he thought Canadian involvement should be voluntary. While many Francophones agreed with Bourassa, many Anglophones

Henri Bourassa Dies

grew angry. They threw eggs and vegetables at him when he spoke publicly in Ottawa. He continued his opposition to conscription during World War II. While a passionate supporter of French rights across the country, Bourassa never favoured Quebec separation. Instead, he worked for a united Canada, independent of British rule. Henri Bourassa died in Outremont, Quebec, in 1952.

1954

Thomas Costain publishes *The White and the Gold*, a history of New France.

1955

The Canadian Sports Hall of Fame opens to honour Canadian French and English athletes.

1950s

Where French and English Come Together

Hockey is a source of pride among French- and English-speaking Canadians alike. Whether cheering for different teams or sitting side-by-side in the same jerseys, the love of hockey is something both Francophone and Anglophone Canadians can agree on. One of the most enduring rivalries in hockey is between the Toronto Maple Leafs and the Montreal Canadiens. The Leafs have won the Stanley Cup 13 times, while the Canadiens have claimed a record 24 championships. The storied rivalry between these two clubs goes back to the first National Hockey League season. In 1918, Toronto skated away with the Stanley Cup after defeating Montreal in the playoffs. The rivalry between the English and French metropolises and their hockey teams exploded in the 1950s and 1960s. In 13 seasons from 1956 to 1969, Toronto and Montreal combined for 12 Stanley Cup championships. The Toronto-Montreal rivalry has been heightened by several trades between the two teams. George Hainsworth, Frank Mahovlich, and Jacques Plante are just a few of the players who have switched sides over the years. This generally causes an uproar among the teams' fans.

Where French and English Come Together

1956

René Lévesque hosts *Point de Mire,* a television show that discusses nationalism and Quebec sovereignty.

1957

The Alliance Laurentienne becomes the first group to work for Quebec independence.

1959

Maurice Duplessis Dies

Maurice Le Noblet Duplessis was born April 20, 1890, in Trois-Rivières, Quebec. After studying law at the University of Montreal, he returned to his hometown to work. In 1927, Duplessis ran for public office as part of the Conservative Party of Quebec. He won a seat in that election. In 1931, Conservative leader Camillien Houde lost his seat. The party chose C.E. Gault to replace Houde, but Gault resigned in 1932. At the party's 1933 convention, Duplessis won the leadership of the Conservative Party. After an unsuccessful bid for the premiership in 1935, Duplessis's Conservative Party joined with the nationalist party, Action libérale nationale (ALN). This resulted in the founding of Union Nationale party in 1936. Duplessis won

Maurice Duplessis Dies

the provincial election that year, putting an end to to the Liberal Party's 39-year reign. With Canada's reluctance to enter World War II in 1939, Duplessis thought the time was right to call an election, but he lost. Duplessis was re-elected as premier in 1944, however, and served for the next 15 years. A strict conservative, Duplessis disliked labour unions and

worked to prevent worker strikes. He was accused of vote-fixing and corruption during this time. Duplessis adopted an official flag for Quebec, the *Fleur de Lis*. Duplessis was still premier when he died on September 7, 1959. Soon after, the Liberal Party regained control of the province, beginning a period known as the Quiet Revolution.

Into the Future

Many Canadians believe their differences bring them together. They often see meeting someone who has different beliefs, customs, or language as an opportunity to learn from that person. Think about the things you enjoy doing. Maybe you enjoy sports, such as hockey. You might be interested in art or music. Do you enjoy going to the movies or reading fiction? Pick something you are interested in, and use it to explore Canada's other official language. Imagine what you will find.

1958
Jean Charest is born in Sherbrooke, Quebec.

1959
Quebec premier Maurice Duplessis dies in office on September 7.

1960
Louis Robichaud becomes the first elected Acadian premier of New Brunswick.

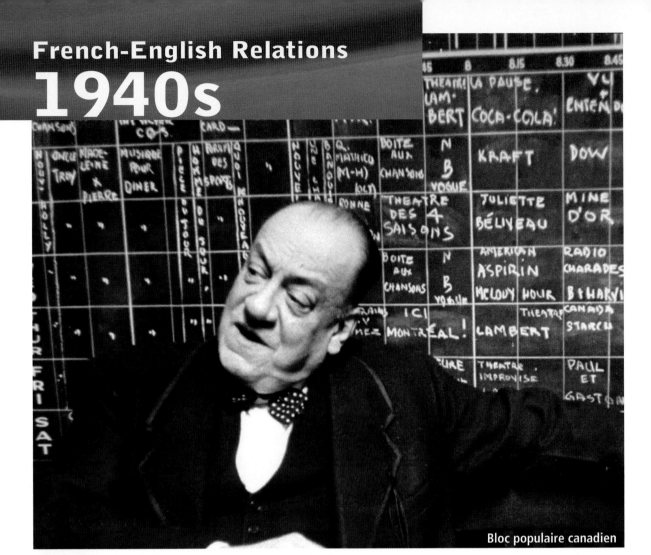

Bloc populaire canadien

1942

Bloc populaire canadien

In the spring of 1942, Parti Canadien founder Liguori Lacombe finish strongly in two by-elections on an anti-conscription platform. This inspired the founding of the Bloc Populaire Canadien in September 1942. The party ran candidates in both provincial and federal elections. The party was inspired by the ideas of Henri Bourassa and his struggle for French-Canadian rights. The Bloc populaire did well in Quebec provincial elections and had strong support from Montreal's Mayor Camillien Houde. At the federal level, party members included Jean Drapeau and Pierre Elliott Trudeau. The Bloc populaire's motto in English was "Canada for Canadians (not for the British) and Quebec for Quebecers (not for English Canadians)." In Quebec, the party won four seats in 1944 and was an outspoken opponent of Premier Maurice Duplessis. In the 1945 federal election, the Bloc populaire ran 35 candidates, all on the anti-conscription issue. Two were elected as members of Parliament. With the end of World War II in 1945, the party's concerns were gone. The provincial party dissolved in 1947, followed by the federal party in 1949.

1941

British Prime Minister Winston Churchill gives his famous "some chicken, some neck" speech in Ottawa.

1942

Most English Canadians vote in favour of conscription, while most French Canadians vote against it.

1944

Conscription Crisis

Canada declared war on Germany on September 10, 1939. However, Germany overran France before any Canadian troops could enter combat. In the 1940 election, Prime Minister Mackenzie King promised to limit Canada's involvement in the war. In April 1942, King asked Canadians to allow the government to take back its promise if needed.

He described the situation as, "not necessarily conscription but conscription if necessary." The idea of conscription was a controversial subject. Most English-speaking Canadians supported the proposal, with 80 percent in favour. In Quebec, however, where anti-conscription supporters such as Henri Bourassa felt the war was not Canada's to fight, 72.9 percent of the voters were against the proposal. One area of concern to Francophones was the fact that French soldiers still

had to work under an all-English command. Regardless, across Canada, the vote was 63 percent in favour of conscription. In 1944, with the number of Canadian troops in service down and political pressure to replace them, King conscripted 17,000 Canadians for duty overseas. Few conscripts saw combat, and many simply refused to "go active." This created discontent, and, in some cases, **mutiny** among other Canadian troops.

1943

The Quebec Conference to discuss an end to World War II is held in Quebec City.

1944

Maurice Duplessis is elected premier of Quebec.

1945

August 15 marks the end of World War II.

Normandy Invasion

The World War II invasion of Western Europe began on the beaches of Normandy, France, on June 6. One of the most hard-fought battles was on Juno Beach, the second most heavily defended German site. It was there that the 3rd Canadian Division broke through the German line. In the first hour of the attack, the Canadians lost 50 percent of their troops. By the end of the day, the Canadians had advanced into enemy territory farther than any other **allied** force. In the following months, they continued their advance to the city of Caen, then on to Paris to free France of German occupation. Many of the regiments were made up of French and English troops. A number of soldiers came from the area of Miramichi, New Brunswick. Many men said they felt closer to the men in their regiment than to their own families. Soldiers relied on one another to survive. This created a strong bond between soldiers who served together. The war they were fighting was a common cause that went beyond language or culture. Of those that survived the war, many remained friends for the rest of their lives.

Normandy Invasion

1946

Arthur R.M. Lower publishes *Colony to Nation*, which explores Canada's two nations within a nation.

1947

Gilles Duceppe, politician and future leader of the Bloc Québécois, is born on July 22.

Labour and Politics

When Quebec asbestos miners walked off the job in February 1949, they set in motion a series of events that would change French-English relations and the political landscape of the province. The miners were fighting for more rights, safer working conditions, and a pay raise. The American and English-Canadian mine owners would not give in to their demands. Eventually, the 5,000 workers seized the town of Asbestos, Quebec, after learning the mine owners had plans to hire replacement workers. The miners even took police officers hostage. The strike was illegal, and Premier Maurice Duplessis supported the mine owners. Most of the Catholic Church, however, sided with the workers and delivered a plea to its followers to donate funds to help the miners. Police eventually threatened to shoot at the workers. Finally, with their labour **unionist** Jean Marchand, the miners began negotiating with the mine owners and were soon back to work, though with little gain. Pierre Trudeau was a reporter covering the events. He would later become prime minister of Canada. This story affected his political views, as he agreed with the workers' request. Trudeau later said the strike was one of the primary events that led to the Quiet Revolution. Media coverage of the strike raised concerns about many of the government's practices. Trudeau, Jean Marchand, and Gérard Pelletier, another journalist covering the event, came to be known as the "three wise men" and would go on to reshape the idea of Quebec federalism.

Labour and Politics

Into the Future

The United Nations (UN) was founded in 1945, following the end of World War II. It sought to promote peaceful solutions to world conflicts and to ensure the world never again went to war. Prime Minister William Mackenzie King was one of the UN's founding members. He helped establish the UN Security Council. Canada has a long history of serving in these forces. What are some of the ways you see countries working for peace in the world today?

1948
French-Canadian Louis Saint Laurent becomes prime minister.

1949
Asbestos workers in Quebec go on strike to demand better rights.

1950
Radio-Canada sends correspondent René Lévesque to cover the Korean War.

Jacques Parizeau

1931

The Beauharnois Scandal creates uncertainty in the federal Liberal Party and its leader, Mackenzie King.

1932

Henri Bourassa leaves *Le Devoir*.

Jacques Parizeau

Jacques Parizeau was an economist and passionate Quebec sovereigntist. He was born on August 9, 1930, in Montreal, Quebec. Educated in London, England, Parizeau earned a doctorate degree from the London School of Economics. He became an important advisor to the Quebec government in the 1960s during the Quiet Revolution. Parizeau joined the Parti Québécois on September 19, 1969, fully embracing Quebec sovereignty. When PQ leader René Lévesque was elected premier of Quebec in 1976, he appointed Parizeau his minister of finance. Parizeau supported the Charter of the French Language of 1977, which restricted English-language presence in Quebec. He was also instrumental in pushing for the 1980 Quebec referendum on sovereignty. By 1984, Premier Lévesque began to soften his stance on Quebec separation, looking more toward compromise with the federal government. Parizeau resigned from the party over this change of attitude. Lévesque himself retired soon after and was replaced by Pierre-Marc Johnson. However, Johnson lost the election in 1985, and Parizeau was elected as the PQ party leader on March 19, 1988. In 1995, Parizeau called a referendum on Quebec separation. The referendum was defeated, but only by a few thousand votes. Parizeau resigned as leader of the PQ and premier of Quebec the day after the referendum vote. He was replaced by Lucien Bouchard.

1933

Robert Bourassa

Montreal native Robert Bourassa served two terms as Quebec's premier. Bourassa was first elected as a member of the legislative assembly of Quebec in 1966. On January 17, 1970, he won the leadership of the Quebec Liberal Party. Bourassa's main focus was to reduce unemployment in Quebec through job creation. He was a young premier, new on the job, when the October Crisis of 1970 began. Bourassa had to ask the federal government to invoke the War Measures Act to resolve the issue. In his second term, Bourassa worked closely with Canadian Prime Minister Brian Mulroney to patriate the Constitution. The agreement that would have made the Constitution law was known as the Meech Lake Accord of 1987. The accord ultimately failed in 1990. The Charlottetown Accord, which was another attempt to amend the Constitution to gain Quebec's support, was likewise defeated in 1992. Throughout Bourassa's political career, he was a champion of the Quebec people, yet he was seen as a moderate voice for balance with English-speaking Canadians.

Robert Bourassa

1933

Robert Bourassa is born on July 14.

1934

Jean Chrétien is born on January 11.

1935

The Action libérale nationale and Quebec Conservatives make a truce in order to defeat the Liberal Party.

35

Canadian Broadcasting Corporation

On November 3, 1936, the Canadian Broadcasting Act turned the Canadian Radio Broadcasting Commission into a **crown corporation**. CBC was formed. It remains the longest running broadcast network in Canada. CBC began with an English-speaking radio service. Its French language equivalent, Radio-Canada, followed soon after. CBC became a tool to bring Canadians, French and English, together. In 1941, CBC introduced its own national news service. One of its first announcers was Lorne Green, who was known as "the Voice of Doom." He covered many events of the war, including the Battle of Normandy. CBC began to broadcast television on September 6, 1952. As more households acquired television sets, programming increased, both in English and in French. Today, CBC Television and CBC News Network offer English-language news and general broadcasting services, while Télévision de Radio-Canada and le Réseau de l'information offer the same programming in French.

Canadian Broadcasting Corporation

1936

The Union Nationale party of Quebec is formed with the goal of gaining more power for Quebec while remaining a part of Canada.

1937

Maurice Duplessis and his Union Nationale party sweep to power.

The Language of War

Canada entered World War II with several French-speaking regiments. Units such as the Royal 22e Régiment, Les Fusiliers Mont-Royal, the Régiment de Maisonneuve, and the Régiment de la Chaudière all served valiantly in the war effort. While these soldiers all spoke French, the Canadian Armed Forces was English-speaking for the most part. All radio communications were in English, and very few commanding officers spoke French. As a result, the French-speaking units had to join larger English-speaking divisions overseas. Many of the French troops felt that if their units were combined into one large brigade, it would have helped lend support to recruiting efforts in Quebec. An entirely

The Language of War

French-speaking brigade would have been a source of pride for Francophone soldiers and Quebecers at home. Instead, the French-speaking regiments were combined with English-speaking regiments and spread throughout the military forces. This practice would later be a key factor in Quebec's opposition to conscription.

Into the Future

The 1930s was a period of great change. Canadians experienced a difficult economic recovery and a looming European war. However, Canadians felt it was right to help their European allies and entered World War II to help. Many Canadian men and women sacrificed their lives to keep Europe and the rest of the world free from tyranny. Their bravery, particular on the battlefields of France, was legendary. Many of these soldiers did not share a language or a culture with France. They were there as allies and friends. Can you think of a time when you have been called upon to help a friend, or maybe even a stranger? What do you think is important in an ally or a friend?

1938

Future separatist leader Lucien Bouchard is born in Saint-Cœur-de-Marie, Quebec.

1939

On September 10, Canada declares war on Germany.

1940

The Canadian government conscripts citizens for military service at home.

Université de Montréal

1920

Université de Montréal

On February 14, 1920, the institution that would become the Université de Montréal, or University of Montreal, was founded by the Quebec government. The Francophone university is comprised of 13 faculties, more than 60 departments, and has two affiliated schools, *École Polytechnique*, or "School of Engineering," and the business school, HEC Montréal. The university offers more than 650 undergraduate and graduate programs and 70 doctoral programs. In the 1950s and 1960s, following the Quiet Revolution, university education was considered an important aspect of a productive economy and a just society. When the university was founded, it lacked the funding that was available to Anglophone schools. This, along with the general poverty of many French Canadians, meant the university had to struggle to survive. However, it eventually grew in size and strength. During the 1940s, the university was a major research centre for nuclear science. Today, it is the largest research institution in Quebec, and the third largest in the country. A centre for political change and enlightenment, the university has a number of distinguished alumni, including former Quebec Premiers Robert Bourassa, Maurice Duplessis, Jacques Parizeau, as well as former Prime Minister Pierre Elliott Trudeau.

1921

Pierre Laporte, who would later be kidnapped and killed by the FLQ, is born on February 25.

1922

In recognition of Canada's role in the Battle of Vimy Ridge, France gives the land around battleground to Canada.

Canada Fights for Independence

Independent Provinces Throughout Canada

The idea of separation from Canada is not just a Quebec issue. Throughout Canada's history, many English-speaking provinces have also pushed for sovereignty. On January 17, 1924, members of the United Farmers of Alberta held their annual general meeting. It was a chance to discuss issues ranging from the price of grain to the lack of clean water in rural areas. The West has a long history of feeling separated from the rest of Canada. A motion was made to approve British Columbia, Alberta, Saskatchewan, and Manitoba's separation from Canada. A vote was held, and the motion was defeated, but not before a heated debate.

Canada Fights for Independence

Prime Minister Mackenzie King put much effort into asserting Canada's right to self-determining governance, especially in regard to deciding its own foreign policies. Prime Minister King attended the 1923 Imperial Conference in London, England, for this purpose. The conference was a meeting between the leaders of Great Britain and each of its colonial and dominion leaders. Canada had long been a British colony, and before that, a French colony. However, the transition from French to British control had been difficult. French and English differences came to a head during the the Seven Years War from 1756 to 1763. In North America, the war was fought between French and British colonies. The war ended outside Quebec City with the Battle of the Plains of Abraham.

The British captured the city, and within four years, almost all of the French territories were turned over to the British. Canada then became a British colony, and many French settlers were forced out. Prime Minister King sought to end this era of British control and gain independence for Canada. His efforts led to the 1931 Statute of Westminster, which granted British dominions, such as Canada, full independence in the making and passing of laws.

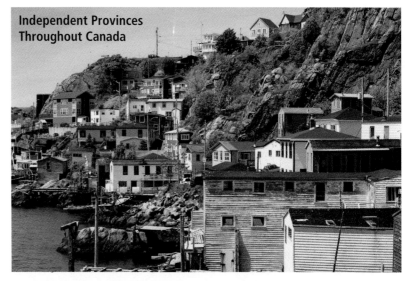

Independent Provinces Throughout Canada

1923	1924	1925
Pierre-Jean Véniot becomes premier of New Brunswick. He is the province's first Acadian premier.	Canadian athletes compete at the Winter Olympics in Chamonix, France.	Louis Robichaud, New Brunswick's first elected Acadian premier, is born.

39

1920s

The Great Depression

When the New York stock market crashed on October 29, 1929, it affected people around the world. This event was the beginning of the Great Depression. With Canada's dependence on the U.S. economy, the country was hit particularly hard. Unemployment rose to 27 percent in 1933, Canadian **export** to other countries declined by 50 percent, and many businesses were forced to close. In rural areas, such as the Prairies, two-thirds of the citizens had to receive welfare to survive. Manufacturing provinces, such as Ontario and Quebec, also faced difficulties. The 1920s were prosperous times, so many companies over-produced in the hope of selling to more markets. After the stock market crashed, factories were left with goods they could not sell. With the U.S. not buying Canadian goods, Canada looked to Great Britain. The British soon became valuable trading partners. The economic strain caused by the Great Depression forced the government to look closely at worker-employee relations. This resulted in the Industrial Standards Act of 1935, which established minimum wages and work standards. The act gave hope to labour groups, such as the mineworkers of Quebec and Alberta. Canada's economic recovery also included the creation of the National Housing Act and the National Employment Commission.

1926

The *Monument aux Patriotes* is unveiled in Montreal.

1927

The Ontario government revokes regulation 17, which had restricted the use of French in schools.

Common French-English Phrases

English	French	English	French
Hello	Bonjour	Do you speak English/French?	Parlez-vous anglais/français?
How are you?	Comment allez-vous?	Excuse me/sorry	Excusez-moi
Goodbye	au revoir	What is your name?	Comment vous appelez-vous?
Please	S'il vous plaît	My name is	Je m'appelle
Thank you	Merci	I do not understand	Je ne comprends pas
You're welcome	De rien	Please speak slowly	Parlez lentement s'il vous plaît

Into the Future

Sir Wilfrid Laurier said, "Canada is free, and freedom is its nationality." He spoke these words more than 100 years ago, yet they still ring true today. At the time, Canada was a British colony, which meant it was under British rule. However, the founders of this country developed a peaceful way to govern themselves. They worked hard to achieve equality and justice for their people, both French and English. What does freedom mean to you? What else are you thankful for when you think of your country?

1928
The Canadian all French-speaking military unit is named the Royal 22e Régiment.

1929
The Great Depression begins with the October 29 New York stock market crash.

1930
Jacques Parizeau is born on August 9.

1912

Regulation 17

In July 1912, Ontario Premier James P. Whitney issued Regulation 17. This restricted the use of French as a language of instruction throughout the province. Under the regulation, French instruction was decreased after the first two years of school and banned entirely after the fourth year. French Canadians were outraged. Henri Bourassa founded a Quebec newspaper, *Le Droit*, in 1913 to publicly oppose the regulation. Public rallies and protests were staged. This regulation was seen as another attempt to suppress French culture in Canada and further damaged French-English relations.

Regulation 17 was amended in 1913 to force Ontario school boards to comply. In 1915, the provincial government appointed a commission to oversee the implementation of the regulation. However, the commission was later ruled to be against the Constitution. Regulation 17 was eventually overturned in 1927. Despite this, the government did not officially recognize French language schools until 1968.

1914

The Royal 22e Régiment

The the 22nd Infantry **Battalion** was formed in 1914 and activated on October 14 of that year. The battalion was deployed to France in September 1915, during World War I. Throughout the war, the battalion was instrumental in every major conflict involving Canadian troops. The battalion was disbanded after the war. However, a year later, pressure from the public and the Legislative Assembly of Quebec led to the creation of a new regiment with this name. King George V of Great Britain later granted the battalion royal assent, making it the Royal 22nd Regiment. In 1928, its French name, the Royal 22e Régiment, was made official. The Royal 22e Régiment continues to serve Canada today. It is the largest regiment in the Canadian army and is the best-known military Francophone organization. The Royal 22e Régiment is also the local infantry regiment in Quebec.

1915

Strain Over the War Effort

Throughout World War I, the Canadian government continued to lend its support to Great Britain in the form of nearly 150,000 troops. Fewer than five percent of the troops were French. The French insisted they were ready to fight for their country, just in their

Regulation 17

The Royal 22e Régiment

1910	1911	1915
Henri Bourassa founds *Le Devoir* to promote Quebec's interests.	Wilfrid Laurier is defeated in the federal election.	Canada deploys its first French-speaking battalion in World War I.

42

Strain Over the War Effort

COME AND DO YOUR BIT

JOIN NOW

First Conscription Crisis

The Death of Laurier

own language. At the time, all military communication was in English, and French soldiers had to serve under English-speaking leaders. This made many Francophone troops feel unwelcome serving in the military. Instead of fighting alongside English-speaking Canadians, Francophones served with the small number of French regiments, such as Les Fusiliers Mont-Royal. However, Francophone soldiers were not permitted to serve overseas, by order of Canadian minister of the militia, Colonel Sam Hughes. Protests in Quebec and public rallies stressed the need for additional troops to fight the German army. This put pressure on Prime Minister Robert Borden. He relented and created the all French-speaking 22nd Battalion of the Canadian Expeditionary Force.

1917

First Conscription Crisis

War raged in Europe. As the horrors of battle reached Canadian ears, volunteers to fight the war dwindled. Feeling he had no alternative, Prime Minister Robert Borden turned to conscription. The majority of French Canadians strongly opposed conscription. French-speaking soldiers had been treated harshly by the military at the time. They felt no loyalty to either Great Britain or France, only to Quebec. Encouraged by politician and journalist Henri Bourassa, many Francophones staged protests and anti-conscription parades. Despite these demonstrations, Prime Minister Borden introduced the Military Service Act in May 1917. The act allowed the government to conscript Canadians to fight overseas. Borden left the final decision in the hands of the Canadian people. He called an election, running on the conscription issue. Borden's Unionist Party won the 1919 election and began enforcing the Military Services Act.

1919

The Death of Laurier

Sir Wilfrid Laurier was the seventh prime minister of Canada and the country's first Francophone leader. Henri-Charles-Wilfrid Laurier was born on November 20, 1841, in what is today Saint-Lin-Laurentides, Quebec. At age 11, Laurier left home for school in Nova Scotia. In 1874, he was elected to the House of Commons as minister of inland revenue. Laurier became leader of the Liberal Party in 1887, eventually winning the office of prime minister in 1896. Laurier credited much of his success to building strong support in Quebec. He believed in the support Canada received from Great Britain, but fought to ensure Canadians could make decisions for Canada. In 1911, he worked for **free trade** with the United States. Laurier soon found himself in opposition to many Canadian business people who had supported him and the Liberal Party. He called an election to settle the issue but was defeated by the Conservatives. Laurier continued to be a member of Parliament after his defeat, opposing the conscription of soldiers in World War I. Laurier died of a stroke on February 17, 1919.

1915

Manitoba Premier Tobias Norris bans French instruction in all schools.

1917

Aubin-Edmond Arsenault becomes the first Acadian premier of Prince Edward Island.

1900s

Quebec Winter Carnival

1900s

Quebec Winter Carnival

Winter Carnival is a celebration of winter and the Quebec way of life. Quebec City began its annual Winter Carnival in 1894 and grew throughout the early 1900s. As a response to the long winters, citizens of the city decided to embrace the cold and celebrate winter. The carnival also coincided with the approach of Lent, when many Christians avoid certain foods and drinks for 40 days as they prepare for Easter. This made the carnival a great way to relax and have fun before the more serious religious events to come. Tapping maple trees for syrup, tobogganing, skating in the canal, and building snow sculptures became an annual tradition at Winter Carnival. The carnival was held fairly regularly until the Great Depression began in 1929, when the economic crisis forced it to shut down. In 1954, a group of local business people revived the carnival. They introduced a mascot. Bonhomme is a jovial snowman in a red cap. The festival became bigger and better than ever. Today, festival goers enjoy winter sports, dogsledding, canoeing, and ice-sculptures.

1900s

Quebec Liberal Party

May 11, 1897, marks the beginning of the Quebec Liberal Party's 39-year reign in the Quebec National Assembly. This was a major turning point in Quebec's history. Until 1897, the province had been dominated by the provincial Conservative Party. The Liberals held power in Quebec throughout the early 1900s. Notable Liberal premiers from this period include Louis-Alexandre Taschereau, Lomer Gouin, and Félix-Gabriel Marchand. The Liberals remained in power until 1935, when the Conservative Party merged with Action libérale nationale to form the Union Nationale. In 1936, Maurice Duplessis and his Union Nationale party came to power in the province. The Quebec Liberals experienced another historic victory in 1960, when the party defeated the Union Nationale, ending its 16-year reign. The election of Liberal Premier Jean Lesage marked the beginning of the Quiet Revolution in Quebec. This period saw sweeping social and economic reform, as well as improvement to the rights of French-speaking Quebecers.

1902

The Orchestre symphonique de Québec is founded with French- and English-speaking musicians.

1903

Henri Bourassa creates the Nationalist League to instil a Canadian spirit in Francophones.

The Acadians

1900s

The Acadians

Acadians returned to the Moncton area in the early 1900s to begin reshaping the cultural landscape of the region. During the Seven Years War, the British had feared an Acadian uprising in support of France. As a result, the British deported more than 14,000 Acadians from the maritime region in the Great Expulsion of 1755 to 1763. However, over the next several decades, many Acadian families returned and settled in what is now New Brunswick. The city of Moncton became a popular destination for the resettling of many Acadians. A strong Acadian culture exists there today. In fact, Acadians can be found in communities throughout the Maritimes. Several communities in northern and eastern New Brunswick are predominantly Acadian. Because of this large Acadian population, New Brunswick and the city of Moncton have been declared officially bilingual. National Acadian Day, August 15th, is celebrated in many Maritime cities, including Moncton, Saint John, and Halifax.

1908

Celebrating 300 Years

Canadians came from across the country to celebrate the 300th anniversary of the founding of Quebec City in 1908. The city was founded in 1608 by French explorer Samuel de Champlain.

Champlain sailed up the St. Lawrence River in the spring of 1608 and established a fur trading settlement in the area. In 1898, the people of Quebec City celebrated the 290th anniversary of the founding of their city by erecting a 15-metre-tall statue of Champlain. On July 23, 1908, thousands of people gathered near the monument to celebrate the 300th anniversary. Festivities included fireworks, music, a parade, and a fleet of French, British, and U.S. warships in the St. Lawrence River near the place where Champlain first landed in what is now Quebec. To honour the historic event, Canada Post issued eight new stamps featuring prominent figures from French colonial history, including Champlain, Jacques Cartier, and historic sites of New France.

Celebrating 300 Years

GEORGES BAREAU

JACQUES CARTIER

1904

Henri Bourassa pleads in favour of bilingualism in Canadian government.

1905

Canada's first movie theatre opens in Montreal.

1908

Canada Post issues eight stamps honouring Samuel de Champlain.

ACTIVITY
Into the Future

In his youth, Prime Minister Pierre Elliott Trudeau was always curious. This curiosity led him to study at four universities in different parts of the world. It also led to a career in journalism and politics. Trudeau had an ability to think critically and ask questions about the world around him. Developing similar skills will help you grow as a citizen of your country and the world. The best way to learn about the world around you is to talk to other people. Think about the cultural group you belong to based on the language you speak. What makes your language and culture unique? Try talking to people who speak Canada's other official language. For example, if you speak English, become a pen-pal to a French-speaking person in Canada.

Become a Pen-Pal

Write a letter introducing yourself to a person in another part of Canada, such as Quebec. Tell this person about yourself and the language, or languages, you speak. Then, ask your pen-pal about his or her language, history, and heritage. Is your pen-pal bilingual? Does he or she do any travelling to English-speaking parts of the country? Learn about your pen-pal's culture. What does he or she eat? What music does your pen-pal listen to? What films does he or she like to watch? What does your pen-pal know about French-English relations in Canada. Remember to tell your pen-pal about yourself and your ideas about French-English relations.

FURTHER
Research

Many books and websites provide information about French-English relations. To learn more about this topic, borrow books from the library, or surf the Internet.

Books

Most libraries have computers that connect to a database for researching information. If you type in a key word, you will be provided with a list of books in the library that contain information on that topic. Non-fiction books are arranged numerically, using their call number. Fiction books are organized alphabetically by the author's last name.

Websites

To learn more about French-English relations in Canada, visit **www.thecanadianencyclopedia.com**, and search "Francophone-Anglophone relations."

To conduct your own research into French-English relations, visit **www.plrd.ab.ca/public/v/ellen.vanderkolk/projectroom/ss10-13/ fr.eng.relations.htm**

 French-English Relations Timeline

Introduction:
Since 1759, when Britain conquered New France and took control of the French inhabitants who lived there, there has been tension between the French and English in Canada. In this assignment, you will conduct research into the history and current state of the controversy between English and French Canada.

Instructions:
Working with a partner, complete Part I of the assignment (the timeline). Working individually, complete Part II of the assignment (essay questions).

Sources: *Canada Today* (textbook)
        Discovering Canada: Shaping an Identity (textbook)
        Newspapers, magazines and other library resources
        On-line Resources

Part I:
Timeline of French-English Relations: Create a table or timeline of French-English relations which includes the following events:

✳ Confederation, 1867, and the creation of the Province of Quebec
✳ Riel Rebellion, 1885
✳ Manitoba Schools Question, 1890
✳ Conscription in World War I and World War II
✳ Quiet Revolution, 1960 – 1966
✳ F.L.Q. Crises, October, 1970
✳ Election of the Parti Quebecois, 1976
✳ Referendum of 1980
✳ Failure of Meech Lake Accord, 1987
✳ Charlottetown Accord, 1992 (and national referendum)
✳ Bloc Quebecois

For each event, provide
✳ **a brief description of what happened,** and
✳ **how it affected French- English relations** (was this event positive, bringing the two sides together; or negative, pushing the two sides further apart).

Glossary

Acadians: French-speaking Canadians descended from French settlers in the Maritimes

allied: a group of countries that opposed Germany during World War II

amend: to change the content of a document, such as a law

battalion: a group of about 100 to 200 soldiers

bilingual: having the ability to speak two languages

conscripted: forced to join the armed forces by the government

crown corporation: a business owned by the federal government

export: products shipped out of the country for sale in other countries

free trade: trade without tax or penalty

independent: a person running in an election without being connected to a political party

manifesto: a declaration of goals

mutiny: open rebellion against authority

patriate: term used in Canada to define changes made to the Constitution

Quiet Revolution: a time of great political and social change in Quebec from 1960 to 1970

referendums: direct votes on a specific proposal

sovereigntist: a person in favour of sovereignty, or political independence

unionist: a member of a labour union

War Measures Act: an act that gave the government special emergency powers

welfare: government-funded support for people who need financial help

Index